"This book feels like one of a kind. . . . *Master* grapples with dream and memory: the song of hands in motion and the story of hands in action. This lyric and spare work is like the poet's image of a Rottweiler holding butterflies in its mouth before letting them free. The poems can feel solitary and deliberate as 'a sparring partner dancing to his own music.' They can feel sensual and are poetic as 'the water dripping off his body like missed syllables.' Yes, I could introduce this book using nothing but dazzling excerpts. They reckon with the inexpressible. Beauty is set free from a mouth with fangs. I'm proud to select *Master* for the Kathryn A. Morton prize."

—Terrance Hayes, from the Introduction

"Simon Shieh 'speak[s] the cadence of rain,' reminding us that 'each of us is a scorched page, part narrative, part dream.' A gifted poet, each line is 'an elegant lure.' *Master* is a must-read, and Shieh is one of our most exciting and promising emerging poets."

—Sherwin Jay Bitsui, winner of the American Book Award
and the PEN/Open Book Award for *Flood Song*

"This is one of the best collections I've read in a while. Simon Shieh's voice is at once crisp and singular: his lines are tight, complex, and layered; his language unspools in powerful movements, so controlled and yet full of the devastating grace that precedes a final blow: 'shattering the bone around my left eye / the doctors called it orbital / / my mistake: resting my head/on his shoulder—letting him cradle it in his arms.' The beauty in this book is heartbreaking, brutal. Unsparing in its analysis and deconstruction of power, *Master* is a startling and stunning debut collection."

—Sally Wen Mao, author of *The Kingdom of Surfaces*

"If you surrender to Simon Shieh's *Master*, if you let your eyes grow accustomed to its voluptuous and troubling dark, you will be rewarded with a singular reading experience: merciless in its vision and craft, dripping with muscularity and sweat, Shieh's thrilling debut will leave you breathless."

—Ama Codjoe, author of *Bluest Nude*

Master

MASTER

SIMON SHIEH

SARABANDE BOOKS | LOUISVILLE, KY

Publisher's Cataloging-In-Publication Data

(Provided by Cassidy Cataloguing Services, Inc.).

Names: Shieh, Simon, author.

Title: Master / Simon Shieh.

Description: First edition. | Louisville, KY : Sarabande Books, [2023]

Identifiers: ISBN: 978-1-956046-21-2 (paperback) | 978-1-956046-22-9 (ebook)

Subjects: LCSH: Masculinity--Poetry. | Identity (Psychology)--Poetry. | Vulnerability (Personality trait)--Poetry. | Beauty, Personal--Psychological aspects--Poetry. | Violence--Poetry. | Healing--Poetry. | LCGFT: Poetry.

Classification: LCC: PS3619.H51 M37 2023 | DDC: 811/.6--dc23

Cover and interior design by Danika Isdahl.

Printed in USA.

This book is printed on acid-free paper.

Sarabande Books is a nonprofit literary organization.

The Kentucky Arts Council, the state arts agency, supports Sarabande Books with state tax dollars and federal funding from the National Endowment for the Arts.

TABLE OF CONTENTS

I.

II.

III.

The hand in the dark was my own.
　　—Jean Valentine, "Miles from Home"

INTRODUCTION

More than an introduction to readers (who will recognize the lyricism that makes this a special debut in the very first poem), I want to write a fan letter to the maker of this very fine collection. Where does one learn such vivid depictions of mystery and memory? I thought of Frank Stanford's vernacular surrealism, except this surrealism is as restrained as a rottweiler holding butterflies in its mouth; a steady, steely muzzle holding delicate fluttering colors. The lucid and haunted tone is bound to the specter of the Master shifting between father and trickster, friend and foe. He is part father, part trickster, part shadow, part guide, part foe. The student grapples with the master, the slave grapples with the master; intimately, attentively, and carefully we grapple with the master.

I thought of Tyree Daye's first book. *River Hymns,* I think it's called. It, like *Master,* is a kind of bildungromanic debut. Metaphor is rooted in experience and dream. I thought of Sylvia Plath's shapely intensity. Of course, the biggest clue for roots is in the epigraph from Jean Valentine: "The hand in the dark was my own." Maybe the influences originate in the dark. Like Valentine the images are simultaneously resolute and fluid, resonant and compact. Moreover, the epigraph forecasts the refrain of hands grasping, reaching and probing across this composed yet intuitive debut.

"My hands are cowbells at the bottom / of an ocean,"
"two dark prison cells / filled with gunfire,"
"I crushed an egg in each hand / let the yolk bleed through my fingers."

The hands grapple with inner and outer natures. Among the most resonant questions of the book: "How do you protect yourself from another's hands / with your own?" Rivers, puddles, rain, and water also create a vivid thread of imagery in *Master*. Near the end of the collection, "the severed hands drifting downriver / are the same hands that once ran / through my wet hair." Hands, water, light, and shadow create a thread of lyrical reflection and movement. The result is a book that feels both crafted and intuitive. It is the best sort of debut, displaying an urgency rooted in the poet's mind and body. Questions of influence may be too limiting for such a book. I felt this way reading Ocean Vuong's debut, David Berman's debut, the debuts of Kiki Petrosino and Jane Mead from Sarabande. This book feels like one of a kind. Its subject matter makes this so, for one thing. The poems unfold inside acts of sport/ action—a point of view rarely held by a poet. When hands move "across his chest, finding the pain in his body / as if it is my own," the meaning is paradoxically violent and soothing. The poems inspire simultaneous empathy and caution. The book's structure mirrors this mix of openness and restraint: it reads like one long poem in parts as well as a series of distinct poems. I mean, that first poem is a beast. The second and third poems: beasts. I could introduce this book using nothing but dazzling excerpts: "Covered in milk, you would mistake me for an angel. . . . Though only seconds away from mercy, I am years away from forgiveness." In these poems, mercy grapples with forgiveness; kindness grapples with wickedness. They probe paradoxical feelings of presence and elusiveness: "We never remember the men / who we cannot forget." Elsewhere we read, "Each of us is a scorched page: part narrative, part dream." *Master* grapples with dream and memory: the song of hands in motion and the story of hands in action. This lyric and spare work is like the poet's image of a rottweiler holding butterflies in its mouth before letting them free. The poems can feel solitary and deliberate as "a sparring partner . . . dancing / to his own music." They can feel sensual and are poetic as "the water dripping off his body / like missed syllables." Yes, I could introduce this book using nothing but dazzling excerpts. They reckon with the inexpressible. Beauty is set free from a mouth with fangs. I'm proud to select *Master* for the Kathryn A. Morton Prize in Poetry.

—Terrance Hayes, 2022

MASTER

KINDNESS COMES TOO EASILY TO WICKED MEN

In every ballroom, he is the chandelier. No,

he is the song
that everyone only knows the chorus of.

Beautiful,
relentless.

He dresses as a dead soldier
every Halloween.
In the army he says

you are dirt under the nails
of your country.

My mother wants him dead.
The family of a young
girl wants him dead.

In the pockets
of his old fatigues, a torn zodiac

and a rusted
metal spoon. Never

in my life did I believe
I knew him.
Once

in a fit of rage,
he named every star in the sky
after a dead man. Premature

blessing.
    One night, in a Taiwan hospital
                            a man

      cut my mother open and took
my body out.
          Deliverance.

             Years later, she will tell me
             We never remember the men
                   who we cannot forget.

   He gave me a necklace
        of teeth. He laughs

each time someone says
        the word *God.*
    Every day

                I guess his favorite color
        and every day
        I get it wrong.

     Mercy, sweet throat.
             Mercy, blackbird.

He once wrote a song about me
    in the middle of the night.

             When I sing it, a black snake slithers
        from my mouth.

Who did you say you were?

A priest?

A doctor?

A man
with a drop of red paint
            on your tongue,
no

            the name of a young girl

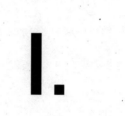

I.

ACT I

Pine-Sol
                on the bathroom tiles
        an offering   to the wrong god.

        Sometimes, I do not see him
    for days.

When he returns
                        a small bird
        dead
            in the toilet means
                            he is restless.

I tiptoe   unplug the vacuum
                    hush the children tearing
        at each other's bare chests.

                            When I am old enough
            he tells me what the mind   can overcome

        and I believe every word.
                    He talks about loyalty. He
        talks about bone growing   on top of bone

                    how to convince my body
                that it's worth it.

        Often I grow sleepy and
            stare at his hair   the gel like blood
                            caked on black fur.

9

His people plant seeds
between their teeth
speak in the cadence   of rain.

                              Though they are solemn
                    he reminds them of laughter.
When he blesses their children
          they offer him their children

    and when their faith wavers
                              in his absence
          he lays his naked back   perfectly flat

on a bed of nails before them and tries
                    not to move—
                                        his favorite

                                                lie.

MASTER (FIVE NOCTURNES)

No. I

Every night we listen
to his favorite songs.
The kind of music you
want to hear when your country
is at peace, but you're told to dig
a grave in the desert sand
anyway, to gather the bones
of your countrymen
like the alphabet of a language
you will never understand.
The kind of music
that might come from a parked
car whose window you are told
to shatter with the butt
of a black flashlight.

No. II

No flashlight. No north star.

I paint myself black and wait for him
with the lights off.

He enters with a girl dressed
in red lace. They dance to a song
she is too young to remember.

In the darkest corner of my shadow
he undresses her
with the tip of an admiral's sword.

The noise she makes, like a flute
caught in a typhoon.

As he comes, he begs to see her
in the moonlight, so I open my eyes—

four bright
crescent moons.

No. III

The earth makes no mistakes.

Caught in the headlights, a deer's shadow
bolts for the woods.

He says our bodies must be
malleable, like water.

I was foolish then.

When he swam through it late at night, the surface of the Pacific was like hundreds
of silk blankets.

He stripped them away
frantically

looking for something.

I filled my lungs with water, sang
songs I did not understand.

I bathed in the low tide, hoping
he would find me.

No. IV

He walks into his house carrying
three portraits, all men. On the stereo
a woman begs a man's forgiveness
to a beat that makes the floors tremble.
In the pitch black, he lays the photos
on the floor next to each other,
scratches each man's eyes out
with a knife, but each time they
reappear—the whites of their eyes
growing brighter and brighter. Furious,
he puts his knife through the stereo
but the woman's voice only grows
louder, more desperate.

No. V

He lights a candle on the table in front of me.
Sickened by my own body, I have not left this room
in three days. Black shins, right eye
swollen shut. In here, no windows, no sky.
To spite me, he hid the moon
in the shadow of a jackrabbit, the deepest craters
in its eyes. When I beg him to show me the night
sky, he slices its body open in front of me, spills
its insides onto the wooden table.

Dark blood glistens in the candlelight.
The body asks a thousand burning questions.

DRAWING OF A SKELETON

He sleeps with the lights on. Night
comes for him
playing a stringless harp.

Branches snap—
the wind licks its broken fingers.

§

After a night of rain, he wakes
paralyzed—his jaw
clenched, his hands, two dark prison cells
filled with gunfire.

§

I learn how to pronounce his name,
how to say nothing to him
with my eyes.

He ties ropes around my wrists,
blindfolds me.
Do not be fooled he says

the darkness reminds us
what we cannot forget.

§

He moves my hand
to the left, moves my foot
to the right.

§

Pain is nothing but the reflection of a man's weakness.

He once told me that
through a locked door.

§

There are birds
in his cages. Untethered.
Faithful.

Winters, he sprinkles birdseed
on the snow outside the bars—
the door wide open.

Their tracks in the snow, sheet music—

a symphony of quiet lies.

§

Let's say I was his.

Let's say he had me.

Is it true that we are perfect
only once, like a poem?

§

In America, a promoter paid him 500 dollars
to kill a bull with his bare hands. They fought

in a dirt stadium—the dust billowing
from their feet like buried stars.

§

He tells me every story twice.

In Japan, a rancher paid him 700 dollars to wrestle his bull.

After thirty minutes he burst through the wooden gate, weeping,
cursing the dead in his mother tongue.

REVERENCE

The first night I dream of him
he pulls his fists out of my chest.

I stare at his middle knuckles
until they are the stones laid on the eyes

of the dead. The second night I dream of him,
he almost walks right past me

in his uniform. When he stops, the light is a dim
copper water. He orders me

to attention. He moves like
a burning mannequin.

The third night I dream of him,
I present him with a blood orange

in a crowded mall. He pretends
this is not ceremony, tells me

not to call him *Master*
with so many people around.

I bow to him. I bow to him even
as he walks away.

DESCENDANT

I have not forgotten my vow.

Every morning I wipe the sweat
from the hollow of my master's throat.
At first he can only move his eyes

then, his jaw. On his dresser
stands a portrait of each ex-wife with her arm
around a different child.

I take his left arm in my lap like a mandolin
rescued from a burning cathedral, wonder
if all the houses I burned down

were my own—their velvet skeletons
still blowing in the wind.
He mocks my Velcro wallet, the beauty

of my eyes. He tells me that one day
he will teach me everything I need
to know—how to touch a woman

on a rollercoaster, how to pull the ghost from a dress
floating in a river. I press the muscle
in his shoulder with my thumb

until it softens, move my hands
across his chest, finding the pain in his body
as if it is my own—spine

dripping last night's rainwater onto the mattress,
knees, two locked doors. Finally,
I spread a hot towel over his face

and see the woman he cannot
stop dreaming of. Her hair
vanishing into the air above him

like steam. He tells me that every scar is an eye which,
after seeing too much, has been sealed
shut. And only after I leave the room

does he surrender to the pain.
Foam gathering on his lips, tears streaming
down his temples.

Sometimes, I forgive him. Sometimes,
I forgive myself.

every scar is an eye which has seen too much

For him,
      I kept a fire burning
in a glass cup.

            His secrets filled the air around him
            like smoke.

      Once,
      he released two wounded fish
            back into the sea.

      It was like nothing
I had ever seen—
            red ribbons

                        red ribbons.
            He named them
                  after his two sons, practiced calling them

      back to shore after violent storms.
                        Fish scale,
            full moon.

                        Today, I am his son. Guilty,
                        loyal.

I feel his fingers searching
                  for the soft hollow
      of my throat.

            He asks me
where I've been all these years,
                  says he doesn't

even recognize me now. *How long*
have you known? he asks,

                    finally,

and every scar on my body

                    opens.

Like all men, he promised me beauty.

At the mall, he told me to buy a hat
embroidered with gold letters.

I told him I had no money
so he spit into his palm,
handed me three silver coins.

II.

RIPENING

And suddenly, cleaning the bathroom mirrors
I saw myself
as he did.

Just to be sure
I whispered, *You are nothing*
like a first love
and the glass filled with black fog.

      Early December
almost nine at night.
Inside, the lights
a bright hunger.
      Outside, snowfall.

On the windows
our heat turns
into droplets of water

and I know some things
we will never get back.

Years ago, the doctor told me
I had a high tolerance
for pain.

I did not tell her
how I cried
when he did not touch me for a week.

      April.
My mother peels the bruised skin
from ripe peaches

      any excuse to talk to me.

That night, she will ask me
to take off my shirt
under the bathroom light.

Like a soldier feeling her way
through an abandoned house
she will trace her finger
over my back
with her left hand

her right hand gripping
a knife.

Again, he quiets us   again

                              he casts us

            like a shadow

      at sunset

                  the longest hour

          he tells us

                                   still, traces of a ghost

                                    in the river

                    a gray stone lifted

           from boiling water

                              if we must love

                                    an animal

                      I tell myself

          it's true

       the circle he made

 on my skin

     is still a perfect shape

                it reddens

                  at my touch

          it goes on

            forever

PATRIMONY

But the captor could not eat the flesh of his captive. He said,
"Shall I perchance eat my very self?" For when he took [the
captive], he had said: "He is as my beloved son." And the captive
had said: "He is my beloved father."
                              —Bernardino de Sahagún, *General History*
                                        of the Things of New Spain

I do not know what becomes of a slave
when he falls asleep under his master's gaze.

There is the fear that he will talk in his sleep,
that he will dream of escape.

      In the backseat of his car, I wrap the fingers
      of my left hand around my right thumb.

Dream of being hunted, they say,
and your feet will twitch.

      He tells me I whispered in my sleep
      in an indecipherable language.

Dream of freedom, they say, and you will wake gasping for air
clutching a wingless falcon to your chest.

But I believe he is innocent.

The nights I do not spend with him
I tap piano keys with my fingernails,
listen for his voice in the instrument's
black mouth.

Alone, I fall asleep wearing the clothes
he gave me. The next morning I wake
holding my naked body.

after seven days I hear his voice

to break a fever
        like a glass   of hot milk

to unlearn the body's hours

dressing, undressing   sun-born   grandson
                                    of a minister

in New York my mother   threw garlic
           spring onions   into the oiled cast iron

the oil spit back   a mouthful of rumors

he called the Italian   restaurant next door
                        to order lunch
              chicken parm, wings
      wrapped in tinfoil
one night
     the bat chasing   my hunger vanishes
                      I bite down

his name an arrowhead
               pulled   from a jawbone
                          no innocence
in knowledge   no innocence in
                  absence   if only I'd known

I knew   she waited
              up on the front porch
       a closed book   in her lap
    like the head   of a sleeping child

all through the   night bats

             hunt, blind

                      if he called my name

        would I go to him

     if he confessed

          would I run

TESTING THE WATERS

I.

I test the waters, which is to say,
      I break a fucking coconut over his head.
He asked for it, or he begged. I try not to dwell
      in difference. The hair of the coconut, the hair
on his head. What makes a man?
      My clean hands, my
white eyes.

Your silence as you lie there holding your head.

This is not quiet.
      This is the painting I made while I watched you open a packet of sugar
with your teeth. There was so much white I had to cut the cheeks
      out of three different fish
and set each one on fire just to remember
      innocence.

Were you ever the man I asked for.

II.

Your lover came to me in the night
like snow over a burnt field.

I was in your house. I was wearing your son's clothes.
You fed me steak—too rare—
and I felt wanted.

She ran her cold white hand
through my black hair, said
Your mother must be so proud of you.

SELF-DEFENSE

To be saved   and unsaved.

To be wrapped   in a hotel blanket   under a table.

Because pain   is temporary but pride

will never abandon you.   All those fires   yelling on the sidewalk

and I never once checked my hands   for burns. I am firewood   being cut

in the rain. I am   trying to tell you that I   was young without

telling you why.   That I learned how to disarm a man

trying to drive a knife through the top   of my head before

I learned how to saw   through the belly of a tree.

Back then older men laid me on the floor and I would sleep   like their first wives.

They taught me how to steal my opponent's breath   from the whites of his eyes.

      I learned that when the knife has already begun its descent

      the secret is to want   to die that way—

my hair parted   around the blade   like a black river.

OBSESSION

He tells me to arrive early. Perched in his throat, a raven soaked
in warm milk. Finally, the sky dries into a painting.

I sit on a drainpipe all morning. I am fourteen. I have achieved
so little. The rottweiler next door will not eat. Instead, it catches butterflies in its mouth

and lets them go. School is out for Christmas. Boys walk the tree line
in the distance twirling axes. I press my palm into the snowy sidewalk—

stupid angel. I wonder who saved me. My hands are cowbells at the bottom
of an ocean. *Here I am. Here I am.* Does he even know my name? He calls me *Chinaboy,*

he calls me *son.* My first words to him are *Morning, sir.* It's true, we take the good
out of everything we name. Summers, I cut his grass. I paint his house

black. No, I paint his house the same beige it was before. One day,
it rains. One day, a hive of bees in his gutter makes me their king. He feeds me

red meat. He watches the blood pool in my mouth, laughs at my red teeth.
In his car, he paints my thigh a deep purple

when he tells a dirty joke. I pull laughter from my mouth
like chicken bones. He tells me he had nothing to do with that girl. Nothing.

I don't ask. I bury my hands underneath my thighs. He names me
after the glow of the full moon. I look away from the window. Slowly, I take the raven

into my mouth.

CLEARING THE HILLS

He spends his days spitting sunflower seeds
into a red plastic cup
as my mother worries a hole
through her sleeves. The thumb
makes us human, she tells me.

I have not slept for two days
and in that time
I have seen so much—
a Japanese maple falling
in an abandoned backyard
during a late-night thunderstorm,
my mother hiding grapes
in the pockets of my blue jeans.

One morning, an hour
before sunrise, he sends me running up a hill
with a violin, drives himself to the top
to watch me play. Broken strings, broken
light. He compliments me, says
it is like watching someone undress chords
with his fingers.

Like so many things
he never told me it was a punishment
and I never asked.

As morning comes, I consider the origins
of sunlight. How far it must have come
to get here. How far it would have to go
to escape.

WHAT IS LEFT

One summer, we cleaned his backyard pool
at dusk. He pulled sumac branches from the water's
surface as I held a black garbage bag open
beside him.

The branches floated on the water like bones
arranged in an open casket.

What, if anything, has changed? Luck,
hope, accident. Disbelief, only the imperfect
afterlife of belief. The same question asked
twice.

When I tied the ends of the garbage bag
closed, the sharp branches struggled
against the black plastic.

How much of me did he take and how much
did I give him?

The bag shook in my hands.
It was like catching a ghost
escaping from my body.

Years later, walking past his house
in a thunderstorm, a nosebleed

takes me by surprise. Head
thrown back, blood flows down my neck. How

did he know?
A drop of blood falls

into a puddle at my feet
and slowly forms

his likeness.
Red eyes, red

mouth. Look
I am braver now.

I promised you I'd run toward the fire
so that I could return and tell you the story
of its destruction.

But here I am, returned, having spent one
whole life running
looking for the fire, and another
looking for you.

III.

MYTHOMANIA

I imagine him reading this / telling me none of it happened

Nose broken from a punch, gushing—

I peel a red puddle off the ground
like a wet autumn leaf.

Using the smoke
from a smoldering cigarette as thread,

I stitch it to the back
of the wounded boy.

Even in war, mercy.

After I finish, I look at his back,
admire my handiwork—

a window of burnt glass.

There is the story, and there is that which the story is constructed to hide. Of course, I want to side with neither—

to be the hunter / and the prey

to be Narcissus / his reflection / and the head emerging from it

gasping for air

I want I want I want I want I want I want I want I want I want I want I want I want

—

What happened to me?

Imagine, for a person who has never eaten, never even seen food—how terrifying hunger would be. For years I was indifferent to literature. Language grew in me like desert plants. I did not know how to cook them, so I ate them raw. Leaves, stems, petals, thorns, roots, all—

An abundance of anything only serves to hide the thing in its specificity. In the worst hours of writing, I wonder what it means, in language, to choose. So I avoid the page. Instead, staring out the window in the early hours of morning, I draw a line from one star to another to another—

their brilliance and abundance, so easy to love. What is harder to admit to loving: their swift and perpetual retreat.

I inscribe an image into the poem. In return, it inscribes a revelation into me.

Trust the poem, I'm told. But I cannot help thinking that its syntax is lying to me; that, like the idea of truth, it creates its own necessity

and, like a confession, unfathomable delight.

—

he draws a map of our bones on rice paper / says he can always tell the truth from a lie

—

I scroll up in the document, read the poems I've written

Writers like to say that a poem is never finished, only abandoned. But these poems feel out of my control; they're no longer even about me. Here, this image began as a bruise on my shin that would not heal, now it is a stone shrouded in steam. I check my shin, the bruise long gone, though there are many scars; from what exactly, I do not know. I continue reading—each poem as forceful as the one before it.

How they have written and rewritten me

Here is the truth: I met him when I was six / I met him when I was twelve

Year after year doubt
rooting deeper in my mind: / *is this / this is not / this is not—*

This is not the life I was given.

Am I confused? / Am I telling the story correctly?

For years, he wasn't allowed near children other / than his own

                                                    As a child
                                                    I was shy, hesitant
                                                    unsure of anything

                                                    I played the piano
                                                    until I couldn't

                                                    It was a July afternoon
                                                    I was thirteen years old

                                                    One moment
                                                    I was staring down at the piano keys
                                                    and the next
                                                    I was gripping the rim of a bathtub
                                                    screaming Bach's inventions

As my parents ate dinner at home / I cleaned the school's toilets with a sponge,
listened to him on the phone with his wife / and counted every threat he made

When I finally met him, I knew who he was immediately. His photos were everywhere.

One night, my parents took me aside in the kitchen

        This is your choice, but you should know what he did

Next day, the neighbor's boy whispered something about him in my ear

        The word sounded foreign

                like a dress being ripped open

True or False:

Only the dead can refuse God.

Each of us is a scorched page: part narrative, part dream.

In good faith, Jesus offered me his heart—his collarbones arranged perfectly,
like the first line of a poem.

Unable to refuse him, I wept as he kissed me.

Hallelujah, he says. *Hallelujah*, I say back.

Covered in milk, you would mistake me for an angel.

If I forget fear, I must also forget beauty.

For years I could only write poems about the beautiful, dark forests of America.
And smoke.

Though only seconds away from mercy, I am years away from forgiveness.

I am wrong about everything. Even this. Even you.

—

One night he did donuts in the movie theater parking lot with me in the passenger
seat

    At first glance / all narrative is harmless

    And there are so many ways a boy / can become a man

Every night we took the garbage out to the big dumpsters in the parking lot. We always wore our uniforms, so the kids working at CVS would be curious, ask us questions. We said we were from the martial arts school next door.

When they asked whose name was written on our backs, we told them, *Our master's*

—

the little we know of memory / the little it knows of us

every thought begins / a small puddle / in the dark

and each symbol / its endless meaning / slowly coming into view / like a glacier

I kept a record of his temperament.

Today, laughter

Today, he drove his car through the garden in the rain

I was waiting the storm out in his living room
when he walked in, soaking wet.

He just stood there, staring out the window—
his clothes dripping rainwater
onto the white carpet.

—

The day my mother first learned what he did / I was in his car with him /
halfway to Pennsylvania.

She burst through the glass doors of the school, walked up to the woman
at the front desk, herself a mother, and said, *You tell me where my son is right now*

We moved to Beijing when I was fifteen

The night my parents told me we were moving, I said that I hated them, but as soon as they left my room, I burst into tears—for the first time, from joy.

—

On our last night together, he took me and two other boys to Applebee's. He ordered hamburgers and milkshakes for all of us—hamburgers the size of our heads.

They joked that I would come back a man, that in China my dick would be considered huge. The word they used was *American*.

—

On the plane, I dream of him dreaming. Beside his bed, a burlap bag full of guns— rifles, semiautomatics, machine guns, pistols—

a bag full of black snakes

DAY ONE

Late at night, in my new home, I wake
to the sound of rain falling through a hole
in the roof.

Still, I keep your things close by—

an Alaskan knife, a blue vial of cologne.
I dab it on my neck, the insides
of my wrists. A fly mistakes me
for bruised fruit. I breathe deep,

walk outside to the water's
edge, though I no longer believe
what I see—

that the severed hands drifting downriver
are the same hands that once ran
through my wet hair.

In this new life, I ask nothing of you.

A tree grows out of the carcass
of a deer—its branches thrusting
into the night like antlers.

At your funeral, three women stood by as they buried you
though only one cried. Nobody
loves the living like the dead.

Your scent rises from my skin, gathers in my mouth
like a storm.

I exhale—my breath, a rain cloud.

My whole life, you treated me like a dream
you would write down when you woke.
And here we are. I lie beside your body
in the tall grass. The wolf tattooed on your chest
saunters onto mine, makes a bed
of my torso, and falls asleep.

Its jaws hanging open,
teeth brushing against my throat.

SPECTER

One night
      in Beijing, wasted on cheap
beer, I roamed the half-lit streets
            looking for him

Here / every night is the same
I sit down to dinner / with my family
imagine him walking / into the house
wrapping his arm around my neck / in a choke hold

He laughs / mumbles something
that I spend the whole night trying to hear

And on the seventh day

And on the seventh day

And on the seventh day

I look to the stars for direction
but find only poor men searching a dark house
for a lost child, their flashlights
trembling in their hands

It is not so much
that I think of him, but rather
that only through him
can I think at all

Seen from outside / the shuttered windows of a pulsing house—
dreaming with eyes wide open

                              And I cannot even speak of desire
                  that mute silhouette

                                          its mouth full of light

Sometimes, the lost child enters my dreams

He confesses the sins of his master
as he unravels a spool of red silk from his hands

FEEL HIM OUT

To celebrate his birthday that first / year away from him / I crushed an egg in each hand
let the yolk bleed through my fingers

—

Three nights a week / I take a crowded bus across the city at rush hour

A coach I can barely understand / orders me into the ring / with a grown man

On the ride home / I watch the city from the window / trying to repair the shattered /
beams of light in my head

—

What is a penchant for violence / if not an inheritance

a rhythm / thrumming inside you

a wasp in the heart

—

Sometimes, I think I get what I deserve / Immaculate white rooms / Unbroken mirrors

How they test me

TRAINING IN YIZHUANG

Too poor for Vaseline, they spread cooking oil
on my nose and forehead.

At first I swear
they want my face
for themselves, as they study it every
chance they get.

They gamble money
porn from the Cultural Revolution—
the village beauty melting iron pots

down to scrap metal in a red bra
and underwear. Nothing sacred here
wants to be sacred anymore.

Scars decorate their faces like arrow feathers—
a sprinkling of incense ash
seasons our white rice.

Every night we wring the sweat
out of our only shirts

list the names of men
and what we did to them.

In a fight the question
is never *what* but *how.*

How do you beat a man who refuses to rise
from a puddle of his own blood?

How do you protect yourself from another's hands
with your own?

My sparring partner lies back, dancing
to his own music,

waits for my hands to drop below my jaw.

Some days they are gentle.
Some days they leave me concussed, bloody.

I stumble back to bed, lie on top of the sheets
dripping sweat.

Somewhere, one of them staggers from bed
to bed, blindfolded, naked

his arms and chest still wet
from a shower, muscles like rain clouds
before a storm.

Hands stretched out before him,
he laughs as he searches the room
for my body.

HE SAYS MY NAME

I've gone through the list with him—
he says that every winter was a cheap metal spoon

bent backward in a steaming pile of rice.
So much of what he says is practice

for another language. *I will go hungry before
I let them win*, he tells me.

In a movie we watched in the internet café
American boys didn't go to school

because of snow. The pine trees looked
so heavy to him—their branches, white stanzas

written overnight. He asked me
how to say *white* in English. Then, *corn*.

In his hometown, they lay hundreds of ears
on the roads to dry. So many that cars can't drive.

Here in the city he sells cigarettes to his old
friends, now in high school. Sometimes

they try to cheat him. Once, he wrestled a boy
to the floor and held him down while I pried

fourteen yuan from his fist, our lit cigarettes scattered
on the pavement, praying for us

under their breath.
Everyone here says they'd rather

forget. Everyone here
wears their own ornament made of flesh

and bone. I've stopped trying to make
them laugh. Look, instead of a house, a pig

under a roof. Look, a window with
nothing inside it but stars.

He asks me to teach him words
while we spar: *knuckle, elbow.*

I lie to him, tell him a *man*
is not a *country*, that a *small heart*

is not *vigilant.* He tells me his favorite food
is *western melon. Watermelon,* I tell him.

Later, in the shower, he tries to pronounce
my English name: *salmon, semen.*

I laugh at his stammering—the water dripping off his body
like missed syllables.

THE QUEEN'S BIRTHDAY, BANGKOK (2011)

Hands resting on the back of a chair, fingers splayed open / palms licked clean

Nothing to give / nothing to take

Skin glistening under a coat of liniment oil / knuckles, elbows, knees, shins / bones luminous in the alleyway dark

Every muscle a clock / keeping time underwater

My coach tells me that he is a man / just like me

That he wakes up every morning / and puts his pants on / one leg at a time

In the ring / the referee tells us to protect ourselves / at all times

To convince myself he deserves it, I stare him down / stand toe to toe / give him my most beautiful smile

My teeth at his throat / like a necklace of pearls

The bell rings / and all that separates our bodies / evaporates into the air / like applause

CUTTING WEIGHT

It is precisely the *kakon* of his own being that the madman tries
to get at in the object he strikes.

—Jacques Lacan

In the locker room
at the first sight of spring
I collect water
from the ice melting on my hair
and eyelashes, weigh it
against my body.

Unsatisfied
I bathe in salt,
decorate my skin with wet black hair and hope
someone will find me.

I would hunger his body
in frayed red rope,
hide the first rosebud of the season
in his waistband
and teach myself to want it—

such is sadness.
When a man does not know his own
he plants it in another's body
and waits.

When it becomes pain
he harvests—

both men down on their knees.

RECORD

In violence / there is no reciprocity
like rain on soil

Shanghai / 18 years old / Winner by knockout

The doctor called a stop
to the fight when he noticed
part of the skull exposed
next to his eyebrow—
a piece no bigger than an eye

Thailand / 19 years old / Winner by knockout

My lower lip gushing
I drop him with an uppercut
as his Queen looks on—
her lips, bright red, her mouth
curled into a smile

Brazil / 20 years old / Loser by knockout

One night before
hoodie drenched in sweat
10 lbs. in two hours

then newspapers soaked through with grease
endless slices of watermelon at the churrascaria

then his knee
shattering the bone around my left eye
The doctors called it orbital

My mistake: resting my head
on his shoulder—letting him cradle it in his arms

And to think
all those years / and not a moment of pain

To hide from the dead / To be with the living

A laugh so genuine

it splits the body in two.

Incense ash on the altar

turns to black paint in the rain—

desire

making time concrete.

In Beijing

the basement of every apartment building

is a bomb shelter converted

into a marriage bed.

It is as simple

as this life and the next.

Simple as a joke

about intimacy

about touch.

The summer I went a month

without touching myself

filled with dreams of candles

burning down like bomb fuses.

I'd wake suddenly

go to the window—

light from the street lamps

grazing my body

like the thinnest silk.

With a dirty rag

I'd clean myself

again and again

watch nobody walk

past the window

like a sea of ghosts

lighting candles in the rain.

ABSOLUTION

I walk to the river empty-
handed

except for a cup
of coffee, whisper

into the dark, forgive me
my manhood.

I pour the coffee
into the river

but only the milk
spills out

splashes into the water
like a bolt of lightning.

No matter how hard I try
I cannot see all

of the dark at once.
And I know

how the sky lies to us
in the rain.

But the snow,
the snow must be a confession.

SELF-PORTRAIT

The hair of the living no different
than the hair of the dead.

He writes poems in the sky with twigs
of burning rosemary. What I have

that he doesn't: a face.
I forgive myself—

floating on the surface
of the water face up as my shadow
sinks to the bottom. *Sweet boy*

you will be good at nothing.

When he blows a kiss toward the camera, snowflakes
billow from his lips. Night cowboy.

Snow hour. To shake a garden snake
from a pile of dead leaves and branches,

to think I have finally found myself
beneath all this skin.

Should the wind be wild—
paraphrase, rebuild.

The opposite of a clock hanging on the wall,
a crucifixion.

I found him naked, spread-eagle on the bed.
But I was filming, so he was gentle.

In his hands, the camera lens was a puddle of rainwater
in the desert. This year, no clouds.

This year, he pulls a bouquet
of lilies out of his car, throws them on the concrete.

They shatter like stained glass.

As he sleeps, I search his face
for resemblance,

but it is as I feared—ripples only,
the occasional wave.

NOTES

These poems are not about what happened to me; they are about the process of writing what happened to me. Their subject is neither I nor he but the conditions of the possibility of writing.

This is to say that I do not believe in confession, for every word speaks twice: once for the master and once to itself, to its own impossibility. I wrote these poems because I was unable to articulate what he did to me.

These poems are testimony. They testify against the master.

—

Perhaps every word, every writing is born . . . as testimony. This is why what is borne witness to cannot already be language or writing. It can only be something to which no one has borne witness.
   —Giorgio Agamben (trans. Daniel Heller-Roazen), *Remnants of Auschwitz*

When the master is dead, everything will begin
   —Jacques Lacan (trans. John Forrester), *The Seminar of Jacques Lacan, Book 1*

Before nourishment there must be obedience.
   —Eduardo C. Corral, "*Our Completion*: Oil on Wood: Tino Rodríguez: 1999"

The shame of being a man—is there any better reason to write? Literature . . . exists only when it discovers beneath apparent persons the power of an impersonal—which is not a generality but a singularity at the highest point: a man, a woman, a beast, a stomach, a child. . . . It is not the first two persons that function as the condition for literary enunciation; literature begins only when a third person is born in us that strips us of the power to say "I."
   —Gilles Deleuze (trans. Daniel W Smith and Michael A Greco),
                                        "Literature and Life"

To the two who gave me life
and the one who made me free

                  —Toni Morrison, epigraph to *The Bluest Eye*

ACKNOWLEDGMENTS

Thank you to the editors of these publications where some of the poems in this collection first appeared, sometimes in a different form.

Beloit Poetry Journal: "Specter"
Blackbird: "Testing the Waters" and "Self-Portrait"
Booth: "Obsession"
Cleaver: "Master (Five Nocturnes)" and "Patrimony"
The Journal: "Ripening"
The Margins: "He Says My Name" and "To hide from the dead / To be with the living"
Mid-American Review: "Clearing the Hills"
Missouri Review online: "Record"
Muzzle Magazine: "What is Left"
Narrative: "Descendant," "Training in Yizhuang," and "Cutting Weight"
Passages North: "Kindness Comes Too Easily to Wicked Men"
Poetry: "Act I"
Poetry Northwest: "Mythomania" pages 43-46 published as "Mythomania"
Rivet: "Self-Defense"
Shenandoah: "Drawing of a Skeleton"
Southern Humanities Review: "Day One"
Spillway: "every scar is an eye which has seen too much"
Split Lip: "Mythomania" pages 48-49 published as "Unforgiven"
Tupelo Quarterly: "Reverence"

"Master (Five Nocturnes)" and "Patrimony" were republished as "Master" by *Poetry Daily*.

"Kindness Comes Too Easily to Wicked Men" was republished in *Best New Poets 2020*, edited by Brian Teare (University of Virginia Press, 2020).

THANKS

My utmost gratitude goes to my wife, Charlotte, for hours spent reading, discussing, and editing these poems with me. You were the first to see, in the earliest draft of this manuscript, the book it wanted to be. These poems are a testament to your words: shame begins to evaporate when we begin to articulate it.

I owe so much to my family. To my mother, whose boundless love and strength bore me through difficult times and whose foresight finally saved me. To my father, whose example I have always aspired to—my admiration for you grows by the day. And to my sister, who I am so lucky to have had with me through this whole journey.

I want to thank my first teacher, Sherwin Bitsui, who taught me that poetry is sacred, as well as everyone who read and provided feedback on drafts of these poems: Sally Wen Mao, Ama Codjoe, Tomas Nieto, Kassy Lee, my workshop cohort at the 2019 Disquiet International Literary Program, Brad Philen, and the first person to read and encourage my writing all those years ago, Leigh Williams.

This book would not have been possible without poets whose work opened the door for my own: Jericho Brown, Eduardo C. Corral, Ocean Vuong, Louise Glück, Terrance Hayes, Lucie Brock-Broido, Thomas James, Jenny Xie, J. Michael Martinez, Danez Smith, and James Wright, among many others.

To the Poetry Foundation, which named me a Ruth Lilly and Dorothy Sargent Rosenberg Poetry Fellow in 2021, thank you for your generous support and affirmation.

To the team at Sarabande Books: I am so grateful for the care and attention you have all given this manuscript. Thank you for taking a chance on my work.

Terrance Hayes, I carried *Lighthead* with me everywhere I went for two years. I've read your poems on a pier on Lake Ontario, in a Buddhist monastery in Myanmar, on the Great Wall of China. To this day I hear your words:

> Yes, I have a pretty good idea what beauty is. It survives
> alright. It aches like an open book. It makes it difficult to live.

Thank you for believing in my poems.

Finally, dear reader, thank you for making space for these poems. I wrote them for us.

JOJO SHIEH

Simon Shieh is a Taiwanese American poet and essayist. He has lived in upstate New York and Beijing where he cofounded *Spittoon Literary Magazine*, which translates the best new Chinese writing into English. From 2008 to 2014 he competed as an amateur and professional Muay Thai fighter in China, Brazil, Argentina, Thailand, and the United States. His work has been supported by a National Endowment for the Arts Literature Fellowship and a Ruth Lilly and Dorothy Sargent Rosenberg Poetry Fellowship from the Poetry Foundation. He lives in the US with his wife, Charlotte, and their dog, Momo. *Master* is his first collection of poems.

Sarabande Books is a nonprofit literary press located in Louisville, Kentucky. Founded in 1994 to champion poetry, short fiction, and essay, we are committed to creating lasting editions that honor exceptional writing.